Through Shimmering Smoke

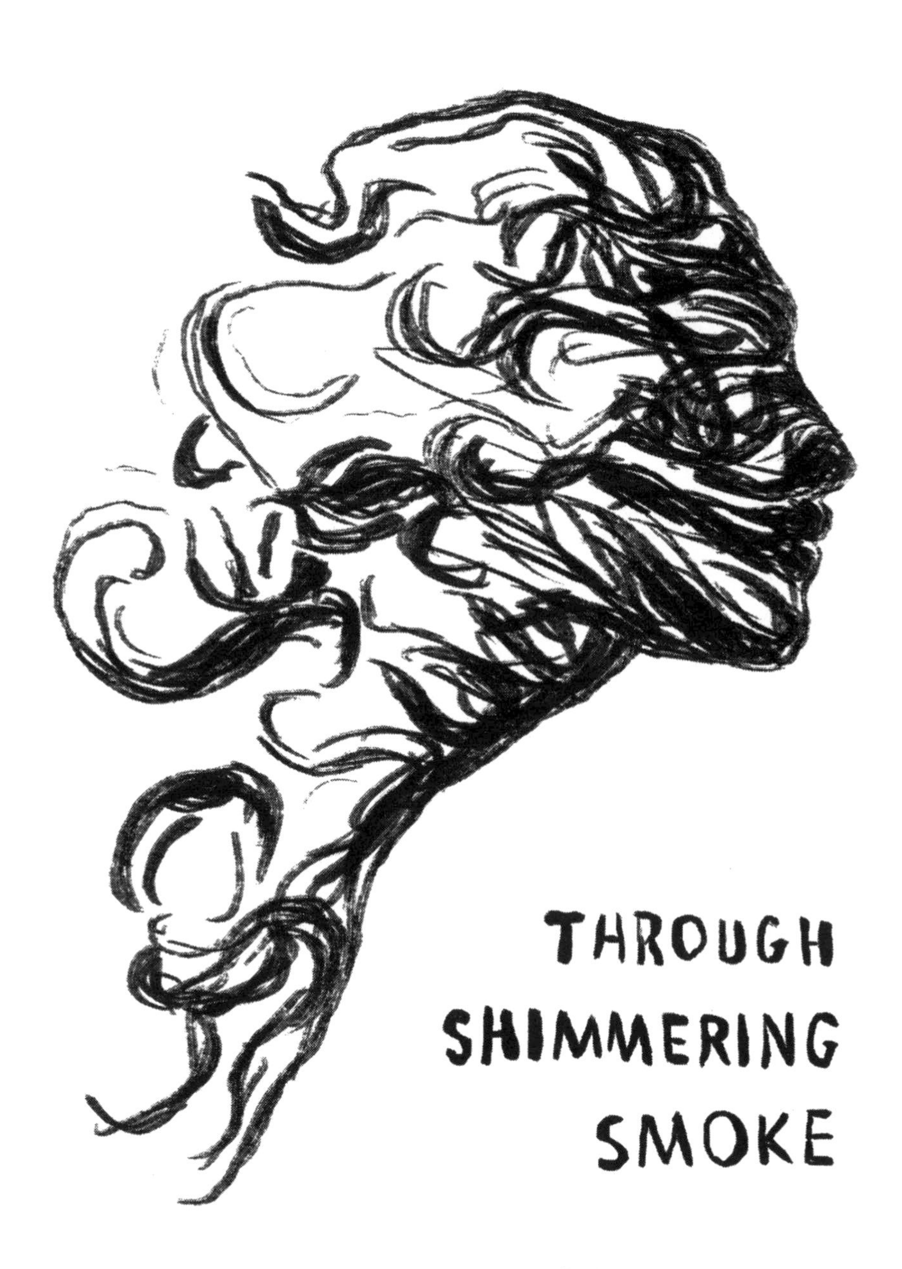

THROUGH SHIMMERING SMOKE

EMMA ROSE GARCIA

throughshimmeringsmoke@gmail.com
www.shimmeringsmoke.com

ISBN 978-0-578-37359-1

Library of Congress Control Number: 2022905296

Edited and designed by Tell Tell Poetry

Illustrations by Jasmine Rain Johnson

Printed in the United States of America

First Printing, 2022

To my mom
for everything.

Contents

Welcome to the Inferno (Do Not Abandon Hope) 3

Where There's Smoke

The Voices in My Head 7
March 16, 2019 9
Let's Rent Bikes 10
Wet Socks 11
Gaslight Flickering 12
Statements 15
Who Knew? 16
Goosebumps 18
Minotaur 19
September 4, 2019 21
Mislabeled 22
Inpatient 23
Nurse 24
Wisconsin 25

There's Fire

The Breakup 29
Confess Your Sins 31
Trust 32
Red Wine 33
Songs That Continue to Sting 34
One-Night Stand 35
Little Liars 36
If You Hear Them Say This, Please Run 37
To My Little Cousins 38

Veils & Vapors

Life After 41
Blinded 42

Bruised 44
Charleston AFB, Building #1000 45
Live or Die 46
The Things the Air Force Told Me 47
Testimony 49
Trust Fall 50
Company 51
Gravel 52
Songs That Got Me Through 54

Whiskey-Lit Flames
Corpus Delicti 57
All Eyes on Me 58
Forrest 60
Cavities 61
Gray Area 62
January 23, 2020 63
Cliff Walk 64
Swim Lessons 65
October 67
The Flood 68
No Contact Order Violation, 10/21/19 69
The Justice System 70
Awake 71
Night Terror 72
Rewind 73
Joint Base Elmendorf-Richardson 74

Smoldering
Bad Days 77
Mantra 78
Shadows 79
Shootings in Racine 80
PTSD 81
Vixi 82
Mom 83

Eklutna 84
"You Are Your Own #1" 85
Hero 86
Grateful 87

Until the Ash Settles

Beginning Again 91
March 2, 2020 92
Bliss 93
Sandman 94
Silk 95
No Question 96
Roots 97
Homemade Wine 98
June 99
Sunshine 100
My Very Clear Sky 102

Important Resources 105

About the Author 107

Acknowledgments

I would like to thank my supportive husband, Jacob, who challenged me to write even when I didn't feel creative, allowed me the space mentally and physically to do so, and built me an amazing office in our home. Thank you for everything, my love.

Thank you to my parents, Andrea and Lou, who crossed the country multiple times in my time of need, always bringing strength, love, laughs, tears, cookies, and probably beer too. I love you both.

Thank you to my brothers, Nick and Jake, for our unheard-of sibling bond. Nick—for the music you sent to me that had a way of making me feel less alone and for our guitar duets. Jake—for the never-ending reminder that you will take my phone calls regardless of the time or the situation you're in and for proving that to be true.

Thank you to my best friend, Paige, who went through it all with me. Thank you for getting me to therapy, for sharing your home, and for continuing to be a person I can count on.

Finally, I would like to thank the Tell Tell Poetry team, who have helped me from the start. In 2019, I submitted my first fifteen poems to you. Three years later, it is seventy-three poems and now I get to hold my book. Thank you for all of your support and resources.

Through
Shimmering Smoke

Welcome to the Inferno (Do Not Abandon Hope)

I hope this reaches someone who needs it.
I hope I can help you feel as if you're not alone
In your thoughts. But let's get this one straight.

This book is supposed to make you feel uncomfortable.
I don't want to scare you away, but I'm going to be
Entirely blunt and unapologetically truthful.

Bullets of tears dried up and formed the ink you read today,
Encompassing the thoughts that circle in my brain,
The worries that keep me up at night,
The flashbacks that take my appetite away,

The depression days when I shit my brains out
After every meal, the days I drive the speed limit
In silence, scream into the abyss, so to speak.

Hang in there because there's a lot of love too.
You better hang in there because I did,
Especially when I felt every reason not to.

Choose life—find a good therapist, eat the ice cream,
Cry when you need to. Hell, cry all the time
Because you are fucking fantastic.

Where There's Smoke

The Voices in My Head

Shiny black Chrysler 200s.
Thick dark mustaches.

Homemade blended margaritas.
Loose gray bedsheets.

What are you talking about?

Betting on the Kentucky Derby.
Hungover Saturdays

Walking around Lowe's.
Jack and Coke. David Allan Coe.

Why don't they sell pasta shells?
We need shells! Hop in the Bronco.

I never said that.

Alaskan boat tours through Arctic glaciers.
Should I buy this shirt?

Did you forget again?

Andrea Bocelli with merlot, dancing
In the kitchen. Pizza competitions.

No, no. Don't cry, babe. Come here.

These moments

Let's take your mind off it.

Are now the monsters

I've done so much for you.

Breathing fire into my bones.

Everything's okay. Don't worry.

With no one left to run to, I believe him.

I love you, too.

March 16, 2019

The night I don't remember,
We fell asleep.

At least, I thought.
Months go by.

It's summer in Alaska,
Iced coffees in hand

With weekend smiles,
Hazelnut creamer.

When the green plastic straw leaves your lips,
Ice slushing around, you say,
We had sex that night.

I say, *No*,
With a chuckle,

A headshake.
No, we didn't.

You look down at me,
Those beady, above-you eyes.

We did, and I knew
You wouldn't remember.

Let's Rent Bikes

It pains me not to know—
            All the unknowns, the answers
Unattainable, the reasons why

            That stay on the tips of fingers,
Wrapped around the mind
            Of your trigger. In the midst

Of all the pain, why'd you take me
            Biking that day? Only to feel
Road rash burning the next few days.

Wet Socks

I remember how your home was laid out—
Where the tile turned to rug,
How the washing machine leaked,
The metal trash compactor that worked (sometimes).

A flannel robe hardly worn, hanging
On the bathroom door next to gray towels,
Gray bedsheets, gray everything.
Toothpaste never capped.

Johnny Cash and Willie Nelson on the wall.
Stained carpet that I was dragged across
In exchange for a rug burn on my knee
That would last for a year.

Gaslight Flickering

If he told you he raped you,
Would you keep dating him?

What if he said it so carefully
That you laughed about it,

Kept loving him long enough
For him to do it again?

Except this time, conscious
Enough to remember.

Statements

As I heal, it becomes harder and harder
To understand my story. How could I
Just lay there and let him do that to me?
How could I just let that happen

Without even saying a word? I pause
With confusion and contempt, then slowly
Realize again: I'm not the same person now
That I was then. I was under his control—

Entirely brainwashed, just living in the shadows.
I let it happen, maybe, because I feared
What would happen if I told him no.
From where I am now, it seems hard to believe.

It's been two years,
Have you found your next victim yet?

Who Knew?

I used to think you were the one,
That I could suffer through your love.
I didn't know that authentic love comes with

Setting alarms to say good morning,
Motivating each other to be bolder,

Stronger, the willingness to learn
Each other's love language.
A laid-back lifestyle where we both

Make decisions, holding our ground
With mutual respect.

When I was in love with you,
It wasn't really love.
It was internally begging for your praise.

It was writing down everything I did
On the days we didn't see each other,

Just in case you asked.
It was never really love
For you. It was loving when

You gave me pieces of myself,
Only when you thought

I deserved them back.

Goosebumps

Dry lightning flashes
Through eyes of rage.

Storm clouds settle
Into summer's night.

Thunder crashes, echoing
Through the weak walls

Of my electrified skin.
Your arms, the epicenter of it all.

I pray the thunder will cease,
Leaving me with rain—

The soft kind, lukewarm,
To help me sleep.

Minotaur

I am trapped in your house—
A 500-square-foot maze I can't escape.

From each corner, you jump out,
Teleporting me back to where I started.

Your apartment, the bottom unit of three,
With wooden stairs that froze each winter.

One bedroom, one bath—my shampoos
And lotions, my perfumes and clothes.

You let me live there. You let me
Make it my own. You let me die there.

September 4, 2019

At first, it didn't hurt. Only mentally—
A silhouette kneeling over me,

Breathing irregularly. I didn't scream.
In and out of sleep, withdrawn

From consciousness, lying on my back,
Gray bedsheets beneath me,

A fan spinning through the darkness,
And a window just slightly cracked.

Waking up was what hurt—
Flames piercing through my stomach,

Burning through my body like a vacant home.
Friction forces its frail walls to collapse,

My mind suffocated by the debris
As it caves in on top of me—

Forcing me down, taking my voice away.
A slight tear trickles down my cheekbone

As I think, *I wish I was still asleep.*

Mislabeled

It was a slow death,
Poisoned by liquid lies,
I drank every drop.

For months and months,
Dependent on you—
Addicted, deprived.

That's when you killed me.
Frozen, paralyzed,
I watched as you murdered me—

The attack I didn't see possible.
Every thrust like a knife
In my back, your eyes

Penetrating my soul,
The darkness of the night
Bleeding into my brain.

I exist now with sudden cold chills,
A tendency to disassociate,
And once-a-week therapy.

Repeating, *I wish I never took the first hit.*

Inpatient

Through black-and-blue eyes,
Rubber furniture, rubber doors
Latched by Velcro.

Can I have another blanket?
Can you turn the phones on?
Can I have my soap?

Cold water. Let it warm up.
(It never does.) Three days
Of unwashed hair. 6 a.m. vitals—

It's time to wake up.
How much did you eat?
You have a visitor.

It was a trap—they came armed
With questions, interrogating the girl
Whose tongue was taken months ago.

Sitting at a large wooden table,
Waiting to pin me down.
They looked down on me,

Thinking my attempt to escape life
Was just to hide from the law.
It wasn't prison, but it sure seemed like it.

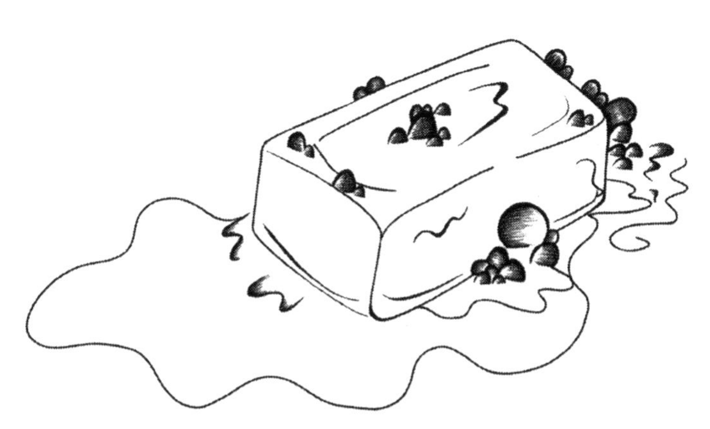

Nurse

She looked at me
With a pale, freckled face,
Dark full bangs, blue eyes,
And a hospital smile:
The police are here.

I asked: *Can you make them leave?*
She tried to help me.
Lord, I know that she tried.

Though, in the end,
It was she who told me:
It's not the first time
A girl did something dumb
For a guy.

Wisconsin

He wasn't a good listener—
He was a good observer.

He didn't accidentally startle you—
He knew how to sneak up on you.

He wasn't upset you didn't remember—
He convinced you that you forgot.

He didn't need time alone—
He needed time with the other woman.

He didn't love you—
He enjoyed breaking you from the inside out.

You weren't dumb for believing.
You weren't blind for loving.

You weren't weak for staying—
You were strong.

Don't question whether he knew—
He knew.

There's Fire

The Breakup

I'm so glad that, last time,
I was knocked out on
Sleeping medicine and alcohol.

He looked at me intensely.
Shocked, even.

That doesn't matter.
That's not a big deal.
Just forget about that.

I looked at him.

It might not be a big deal to you,
But it's a big deal to me.

He pulls the passenger door handle,
Shakes his head,
And slams the door.

Confess Your Sins

Did you tell anyone
What you did to me?

Your friends—
The ones who sniff lines every other day?

Or your mom—
Did you tell her?

Has the guilt calloused your heart?
Do you feel that? Do you feel it?

The throbbing behind your eye?
I know you still see me,

Lying there in your bed.
I'm not going anywhere.

Trust

That was the night,
The one he was waiting for—
The finale, if you will.

All those months
Of getting to know me—

Watching me at work,
Getting me to play on his soccer team,
Giving me a shoulder to lean on.

He groomed me.
He was calculated.

But I didn't know it then.
That's the tragic part, isn't it?
Not until it was too late

And I realized
I'd never be the same.

Red Wine

Wine stains my white sweatshirt
The same way guilt spills down
A clean slate.

I was misinformed.
Dark red and sporadic.
Slowly, drop after drop,

I didn't realize that the clean,
Pure, innocently white vanishes.
It changes you.

I ask, *How did this happen?*
I am addicted now.
I sip the evil with my pinky raised,

My soul unaware of its lasting impact.
I was hopeful I'd never reach
The bottom of the bottle.

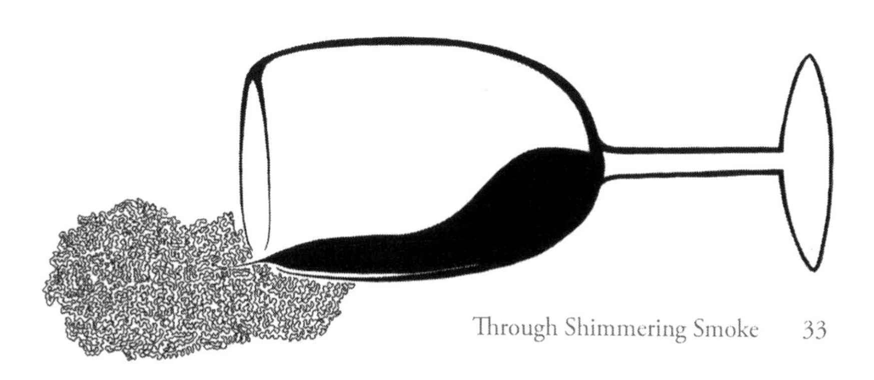

Songs That Continue to Sting

1. "Tennessee Whiskey," Chris Stapleton
2. "Girl from the North Country," Bob Dylan & Johnny Cash
3. "Father and Son," Cat Stevens
4. "Don't Think Twice, It's All Right," Bob Dylan
5. "Bambi," Jidenna

One-Night Stand

Am I bad at love
Or do I just fear commitment?

I've been hurt before. I've been
Knocked out senseless, attacked,

Raped, taped. Now I'm going down
The road of escape, telling myself

It's all right. I use my words to fight.
But you don't listen to a damn thing

I say. I learn to hide the pain.
Now did I run away or leave you

Behind? I can tell I'm thinking
With a whole new mind. Am I bad

At love or do you still control me?
I'm in a new man's arms, but I feel

Like you own me.

Little Liars

Only in fairy tales
Do guys always have
Condoms on hand.

If you're not on the pill,
Then you're a prude.
You won't be any good

Now, will you?
It's just another way
Our bodies are controlled.

Meeting a standard
Men find themselves
Entitled to. *Disgusting.*

If You Hear Them Say This, Please Run

1. *My ex was crazy.*
2. *You have problems and I can't always be the one to solve them.*
3. *I've done so much for you.*
4. *You have no idea how hard I'm trying to change for you.*
5. *We had sex and I knew you wouldn't remember.*

To My Little Cousins

Beware the man who walks around with a cocky grin,
Who smiles and asks you to compliment his perfect teeth.

Beware the man who tells you stories that don't make sense—
Tales of ex-girlfriends and how you can't trust your best friend.

Beware the man who gets in your head,
Who asks for details one could easily forget.

Beware the man who limits your voice
Because *that's private* is the best excuse to keep you quiet.

Beware the man who can never be wrong,
For he is the man they'll never catch.

Veils & Vapors

Life After

I wonder if I'll find peace.
Or will I always be left wondering?

Regret flows through my blood,
Only some nights though.

I wake with an urge to kill.
A storm brews drop by drop,

Like the caffeine we fill
Our bodies with day after day.

Some days I am sober.
I think clearly. I know I did

What I needed to. But what if
I made a call that night?

What if I sat outside and waited
For help? What if I let myself cry?

What if I fought for myself?
Would it be different?

Blinded

Alright, ma'am. Please state your first and
Last name for the record. This is my partner.

He's going to be taking notes while we talk.
Can I get you anything?

My chest tight before we begin,
Digging my nails into the seat cushion

Below me, tapping my toes
On the white-tiled floor, I inhale,

Tasting the coffee lingering on my palate.
You're walking inside. What do you see?

A coat rack, red rain jacket, flannels,
Steam rising behind him, water droplets

Bouncing off his hair onto his skin,
The carpet under my feet soft and inviting.

Take this to help you sleep. I know
You haven't been sleeping well lately.

Looking down at a bluish textured pill,
That's so thoughtful of you.

He wakes me up.

Bruised

Once a rug burn of intimate bliss,
Now a blemish of painful remembrance.

A copper penny with just one purpose—
Reminding me you're still there.

Across the room,
A storm of lust in your eyes.

Shallow breaths of fury
Draped over my body,

Tears dampening the mood.
I glance down and see it—

That copper penny
Below my knee

That would take two years to vanish,
Who knows how many to heal.

Charleston AFB, Building #1000

Waiting rooms, where thoughts harbor.
Shipwrecked, stranded. Casting lines
Into a sea of despair,

Stuck on seaweed and the marsh.
Swallowed by the current of impending doom.
Bleak walls and uncomfortable furniture—

Beige and key-lime green.
No mesmerizing fish in a glowing
Blue tank to keep me occupied.
Would it help?

Live or Die

If you're like me, you fear
That one day you'll get shot.

You fear drowning.
You fear being kidnapped.

You fear you'll never be okay.
Maybe—just maybe—because

So many bad things have happened
That were out of your control.

The Things the Air Force Told Me

They told me not to talk.
If you talk, you won't win.
Be a good victim.

One missing detail
And it never happened.
Wait, you did what?

Oh . . . it's okay.
You lost some points.
We'll still fight though.

Only a few more months—
They found some evidence.
We think we got him.

They believe you, but . . .
They can't go forward.
You shouldn't have done that.

You just weren't a good enough
Victim to convict him.
Now that that's over,

What's your punishment?
You're in what hospital?
Why are you having these feelings?

We'll get you out of here soon.
To a new state, to new beginnings.
It's going to get better.

Don't miss deadlines.
Don't complain about how
He didn't get caught.

Then you'll look bad.
They're waiting for you
To look bad.

Be a good girl.
Be a good victim.
Be a good airman.

Testimony

He said:
I wanted it to be her.
I wanted it to work,
But I can't control myself.

Trust Fall

My mind, a pendulum
Swinging out of control,

Pushed by cunning hands.
I beautifully put together

One thought after another,
Until my husband—

My poor husband—
Thinks I don't trust him.

All because I let my mind
Run wild. All I can do is say

I'm sorry.

Company

Paranoia breaks the dead bolts
Of my brain. The floor disappears.

I have nothing to stand on.
I want to scream:

Get out! Get out! Get out!
But they won't—

Not for a million more breaths—
Not until I'm exhausted.

Gravel

Sprinting to the road, 2 a.m. shadows
Latch onto my heels, tackling me to the pavement.

Help me! Someone, please, help me!
Dragged legs first back into your grip,

While the man on the moon casts his spell—
Taking my voice away. Silenced,

No one can hear me now. It's over.
The road, the cars, the tall streetlight—

I saw it. I was there! I saw it!
Only for a moment though, in my mind.

Brought back to the bathroom mirror, his faint breathing
Wavers around my ears, reminding me I haven't left.

I whisper, *I'm not strong enough. I'll never make it out.*
Exiting the washroom, passing the front door, defeated,

With heavy eyes, blankly staring at the moon,
I lie back down next you. *Goodnight.*

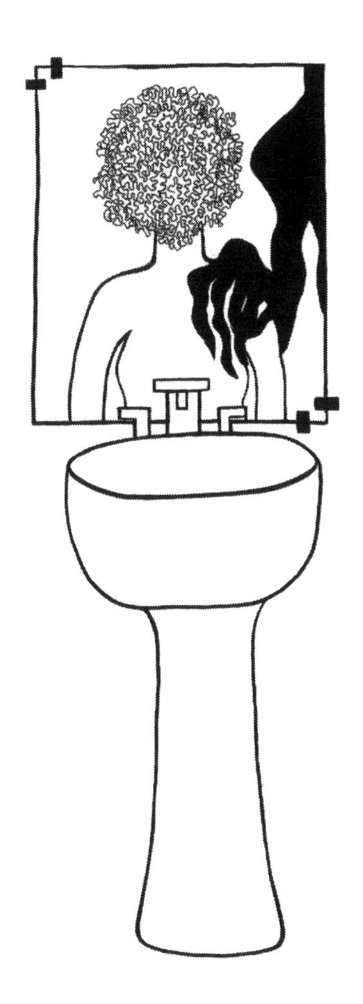

Songs That Got Me Through

1. "Gypsy," Fleetwood Mac
2. "Alright," Russ
3. "2009," Mac Miller
4. "Pretty Little Fears," 6LACK & J. Cole
5. "Train Wreck," James Arthur

Whiskey-Lit Flames

Corpus Delicti

You can tell the most detailed story,
One that doesn't change even a little—
You know it all too well.
But it doesn't matter.
If there's no evidence,
It doesn't matter.

He'll get a lawyer.
You'll say everything,
You'll sit through interviews over and over,
You'll trust the process,
All while he doesn't say anything.

He'll walk away with a smug grin,
A poor-me tear in his eye
(When people are looking),
And a tweet that reads: *2019 man. . . .*

All Eyes on Me

People tell me I'm strong.
Like, how do you do it?
I roll my internal eyes,
Give a humble smile.

I've heard it since I was fifteen,
Since the cameras were found
Under laundry baskets,
And I was found—

The star of a big show
I didn't know was being filmed
For one year,
Naked.

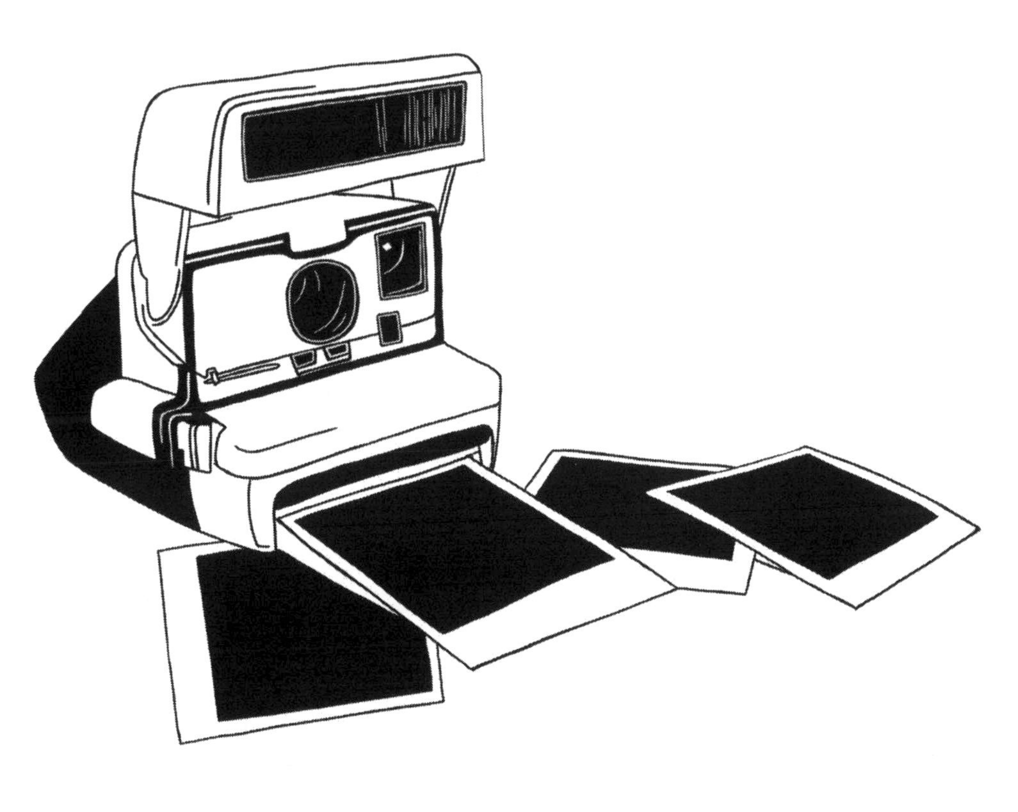

Forrest

She's a feeling stuck in time,
A sunny storm toeing the line.
She's screaming, *Happy Monday!*
While others roll their eyes.
She's six feet under, asking, *Why?*

She's the golden glow come sunrise,
Mixed with falling ashes from the sky.
She doesn't know who will listen,
So she never speaks. Only shares
Too much till everyone leaves.

She's trauma's wounds unhealed,
Surrounded by unconditional love.
She's doing it herself, until she finds the one.
She's looking for guidance from above.

Cavities

I can no longer stomach Biscoff cookies on airplanes.
You were so excited when your sister mailed them to you.

They soon became our morning hangover snack,
Our before-dinner nibble, my can't-sleep little treat.

Now all I see is your kitchen, the look in your eyes
While making me question my memory. The way

Your voice would intimidate me, while your words
Comforted me. The forceful slap of your hand

Hitting the table, as I stepped back, an inch closer
To the cookie jar. I remember all the lies, the moments

You held me, after making me cry. I remember it all
Just by sitting next to a girl who asks for cookies

Instead of pretzels.

Gray Area

There were nights when self-care
Turned into self-destruction.

Bubble baths became drowning.
Just one glass of wine would never do.

And the medication they forced on me—
Tiny capsules of gunpowder,

Wondering: *How many would it take?*

January 23, 2020

So it's over—*not guilty.*
I knew this day would come.
Eventually. I find some comfort

Sitting on the floor,
Sipping my third glass
Of gas-station wine.

Cheers to you! I tell the walls.
Bravo! to the ceiling.
An hour passes.

I don't have plans of moving.
My lawyer calls to check in.
Yeah, I understand.

I guess that makes me a liar.
Because I don't understand.
Would you?

Cliff Walk

Depression is staring at the ground,
Hoping it takes you somewhere else.

It's thinking: *Maybe if I pinch my skin,*
The pain inside will go away. It's feeling

Like you are on a roller coaster while
Sitting on a train. On the worst days, it's thinking:

I wonder if my car can drive itself.

Swim Lessons

A wave crashed over me tonight,
The type of current that traps you

With eyes wide open—
Flailing like a fish on dry land.
There's a choice to be made:

To search for the light above
Or to let myself sink?

I test the limits when I'm alone
And there's no one to help.
How long can I go?

Every day, it seems, I survive
By floating. Other days, I skim

The surface, wondering when
I'll be back on dry land.
Will I be able to stand?

October

I tried—
I tried to end it.
I couldn't.

That came with its own loss, too.
I had my window and I blew it.
I can't try again now. (Can I?)

Some days—
Today especially—
I can still hear your voice:

You should have tried harder.

The Flood

I am numb, exhausted, hollow.
Empty, breathing, but not by choice.

Spinning while laying perfectly still,
After five chugs of I-can't-remember.

Disgusted by haunting memories
Of dyeing my hair brown for you,

Of ignoring my mom's phone calls
And not knowing where to go.

Angry he's out there. Who's next?
Embarrassed that I couldn't stop him.

Confused about what's to come.
Thankful for those who keep me here.

No Contact Order Violation, 10/21/19

You knew what your hazel-eyed
Side-stare would do to me.

You knew it all too well.
But you did it anyway.

You couldn't stay away.
So I tried to stay away.

Was that what you wanted?

The Justice System

In the end,
Nothing ever happens.
What more do you expect?

Awake

My stomach twisted in terror.
My brain spiraling, screaming,
In shame. My fists clenched in fear.

Intrusive images lift my eyelashes
One by one, until my eyes are wide open.

Gazing senselessly,
Watching the smoke detector flicker—
Green, green, red. (Pause.) Green, green, red.

My nails biting into my palms.
Could he come after me again? At 2 a.m.?

Night Terror

Turning left and right, I find no safety.
My body sweats. My vision goes blurry.

I touch back down to the world I fear most.
Would you shave your head just to be unknown?

Perhaps sell your car, just in case he's looking?
Or move to a new state, one he doesn't know?

My back against the wall, I feel better,
Though my fears often come with the weather—

A somber haze that closes in on me.
He's released back to the world—free, no restraints.

What does that mean for me? Am I safe?
The wind comes knocking on my windowsill,

Jolting me out of bed with twitching legs.
I hide in my closet, but he's there, too.

Rewind

She kneels on the concrete.
Nothing is as it seems. A hood
Over her head to hide the disbelief.

She wasn't meant to be a criminal.
She wasn't meant to do wrong things.
Her purpose was to love without

Hesitating. A cold mist and breeze,
Warm red cheeks hold in the pain.
Revenge wasn't meant for the good-

Hearted. I saw my body lying in the prison
Of your twisted mind. Nothing is as it seems.
It wasn't me.

Joint Base Elmendorf-Richardson

It's the way I was thrown around,
Looked at, talked to, shamed

That still bothers me. Perhaps more
Than the mental torture I faced.

It wasn't just the justice system.
It was the military.

Smoldering

Bad Days

—Hey, are you okay?
—Who me?
—Yeah, you just seem lost.

I'm thinking of him—
Sitting in an interrogation room

Refusing to speak, knowing what
He did to me, being too smart

To open his mouth except to ask
For a lawyer.

I'm thinking of him,
Telling everyone that I'm crazy—

She's making the whole thing up.
She's just mad we broke up.

I'm thinking of him—
Spreading my legs, turning me

To my stomach, and rolling over
To his side when he's finished.

I'm fine. Give 'em a soft smile
And go back to my desk.

Mantra

I want to heal—

For my husband,
For my future daughter,
For myself.

Because we all deserve better.

Shadows

There's a ghostly pain
That covers me when I sleep
And follows me when I walk.

Hollow like the walls of a broken home,
Dark as the longest winter in Alaska,
And fleeting like the eclipsing thoughts I used to have.

Though now, I want to live.

Shootings in Racine

I realize more and more how torn I am
In my aching, wondering

About whether you are okay
Or if you are alive.

I can't decide which
Would make me feel better.

Or could it always be worse?

PTSD

I'm scared. The voices have returned—the ones that glue my lips shut. Everything I say will be used against me. How do I tell him? How do I help him understand? I try. I tell him that it's not him—it's *him*. That it's not what he did to upset me—it's what *he* did. It all seems to fail. Did I fail? Screaming on the floor, repeating: *I'm sorry, I'm sorry*. Over and over, until the night is over.

Vixi

An angel came
As I was drifting off,

As my thoughts were taking me away
To rubber furniture, puzzles,

And paper-thin blankets. An angel came
Who turned the sound up to seventeen—

A reminder that I have lived.
I am alive.

I want to live.

Mom

She saves me over and over,
All through my life.

Four trips to Alaska
When the "fun" wouldn't stop.

One large pepperoni pizza—
Just in case you want to eat.

Telling me I look great after
Fifteen pounds fell off me in a week.

Postponing her flight home
Just to stay a little longer.

Making up names for my abuser—
Little Hand Mustache Man was the best one.

(He really did have small hands.)
I had to convince her I wouldn't

Kill myself before she would leave.
I know she still worried though.

She's the strongest woman I know
And I get to call her Mom.

Eklutna

Fog rises over the lake of my aura
As spring sun suddenly returns,

Reflecting off old wounds like cracks in the ice,
Begging to be noticed.

I dip my toes into the 6 a.m. mist,
Thinking this is the year I dive in.

Though no matter how far I dive,
There will always be wounds that seep,

Bubbles that rise,
Never fully vanishing.

"You Are Your Own #1"

—Dad

There are going to be
So many people out there
Who will make you feel powerless—
Like you don't have a say,
Like you're disposable.

But you gotta know you have a flame.
You can turn down plans.
You can quit a job.
You can tell your boyfriend
You don't want to have sex.

You are all that matters.
Your comfort is the priority.
Don't give him three strikes till he's out.
Wear whatever you want to the bar.
Scrape the bottom of that Ben and Jerry's in one sitting.

If he loves you, he won't control you.
If he loves you, he will respect you.
If he loves you, you won't be scared to say no.

Hero

for Paige

A person who is admired or idealized for courage,
Outstanding achievements, or noble qualities.

Where would I be without you?
I would be silenced.
I would be voiceless.

A hurricane of traps and flashbacks.
You guided me through a storm of self-doubt—
A constant light during waves of oblivion.

When I began to sink, you offered me clarity.
Every time I tripped, you let me get up on my own,
Allowing me to grow.

Our storms have passed now. We made it through.
So how's the weather over there?

Grateful

I've been bleeding on paper for years,
I'm not sure how to paint my wings.

I feel all the love in the world for you,
Though I have no words to describe it.

When we fight, I feel no rush
To pen and paper. It's all within me.

My inner voice is calm and faithful.
My inner judge doesn't need a jury.

How do I describe that?

Until the Ash Settles

Beginning Again

I think when you find someone who you're meant to be with, your life begins to come together, effortlessly. Ideas, questions, and decisions all get two brains working in tandem. Disagreements lead to better outcomes. More possibilities are considered and you come to wiser decisions. As I think all of this in a lovely daydream, I'm brought back to reality by our matching coffee mugs gently kissing the table as you sit down. *Thank you.*

March 2, 2020

Charleston

We fell in love.
It happened quick,

Just as winter turns
To spring in the South,

Bringing new light to dark places,
A burst of energy to a life that was stagnant.

I wouldn't change it—
Not for a second.

Bliss

I went from saying,
I want to die die die,

To singing, *Heaven*
Is a place on earth.

Dancing with the puppy
While you're cooking,

Spinning with love,
Reaching for your hand—

Not afraid anymore.

Sandman

No more heartache.
No more *what did I do wrong.*

No more second-guessing
That text I just sent.

No more reading it
Over and over till 2 a.m.

Now I sleep—
Good sleep, amazing sleep,

The kind I've missed
For years.

Silk

I lay a pillow by my side the nights you're away
On deployment, working nights, for training—
A common occurrence in the military.

I line it up so my arm can reach,
Pretending I can graze your chest.
I imagine I see you before closing my eyes.

On these nights I like to imagine
The future, with little humans to keep me
Company while you're away.

No Question

I would never want to flirt
With another boy ever again.

I have you—my man.
That's all I want forever.

Roots

We are flowers in bloom,
The clouds merging together.

We are snowflakes falling
Slowly next to one another,

Effortlessly flowing through
The seasons as independent creatures.

We live in tandem.
We evolve together.

I am still me.
You are still you.

Homemade Wine

She dances in the kitchen to the one song—
The one for joy, the one for aching pain,

The one for empowering days,
The one for blame, blame, blame.

Angelic twirls, open arms, misty eyes.
Pots and pans piled high, spices, and red wine.

"Gypsy"—the one requested all the time.
Poorly sung with wide eyes looking inward,

No worries about who could be watching.
Just bliss planted musically in my veins

Only for me to feel
When I need it the most.

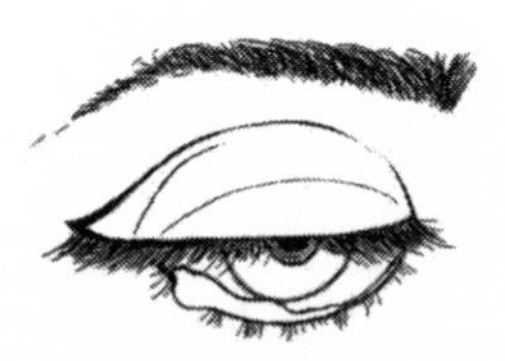
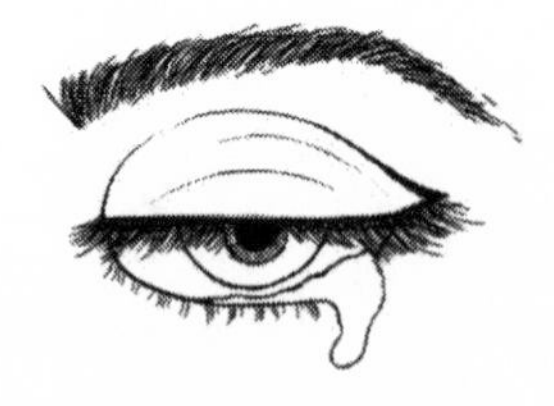

June

Some days I think about
What it would have been like
If I had killed myself.

How I wouldn't be lying here
Next to my husband.

I wouldn't have a home to call my own,
Pets to rush home to. Little celebrations

That life gives me would go unnoticed—
Going home to meet my cousin's baby,

Seeing my mom beat cancer for the second time.
Holidays would have been missed and sunny days wasted.

I wouldn't be lying here
Wondering what it would've been like.

I didn't let the bastards win
And I'm proud of that.

Sunshine

For once, the future seems so clear. The hurricane has passed. I know that, with you, I will accomplish more than I could ever have dreamt. I see it all with you. I will publish this book, run marathons, finish my degree, have kids, build a house—all of it with you. And I'm just getting started. You're the stars I prayed on. You've helped me transform on my own. A simple thank-you could never suffice.

But here I am, saying, *Thank you.*

My Very Clear Sky

Goodnight to the world
I've grown to love again.

Goodnight to my body
That feels safe again.

Goodnight to my mom,
Whose guidance is unmatched.

Goodnight to my husband—
Your love for me is a constant blessing.

Goodnight to those who have hurt me.
If not for you, where would I be?

If you or someone you love is dealing with any or all of the issues described in this book, please don't hesitate to reach out to the following organizations for help. You are not alone.

National Domestic Violence Hotline
1-800-799-7233 (text: 88788)
www.thehotline.org

National Suicide Prevention Lifeline
1-800-273-8255
www.suicidepreventionlifeline.org

RAINN: Rape, Abuse, & Incest National Network
1-800-656-4673
www.rainn.org

US Department of Defense Sexual Assault Prevention and Response
571-372-2657
www.sapr.mil

Veterans Crisis Line
1-800-273-8255 and press 1 (text: 838255)
www.veteranscrisisline.net

Emma Rose Garcia is a self-taught poet from New England, who never leaves home without her Hydro Flask and can only write poems on paper—preferably a leather-bound journal with a blue ink pen. At fifteen years old, she started a nonprofit called Press Pause, where she spoke at high schools about video voyeurism. It was then that she grew passionate about telling her story. It was then that she learned the power of vulnerability.

In this collection, Emma shares her story once more, this time about her career in the Air Force during which she dated a man who changed her life forever. She now lives in a cookie-cutter neighborhood with her husband Jacob, her dog Pico, and her cat Olive. She's thankful for her experiences because they have led her right where she needs to be.

Emma hopes that this collection touches a few souls who may be grieving the person they once were. She prays that her words might help someone to leave an abusive relationship. Lastly, she wants you to know that you are not alone.

Made in United States
Orlando, FL
23 May 2022